GUIDE TO SHELLS

Jennifer Cochrane

Illustrated by Graham Allen
and Fred'k St. Ward

Designed by Jane Olliver

A Piccolo Explorer Book
Pan Books · London and Sydney

Contents

Below, starting top left: Limpet, cowrie, auger, olive shell, volute, chank shell, cat's-eye shell, scallop, tusk shell and conch.

About This Book

This book introduces the young reader to the different kinds of shells that are found in the world's seas. It shows shells of sandy, rocky and muddy beaches and exotic tropical shells. It also explains what shells are and how they are made.

The hobby of shell collecting is an easy one to start, and can make a holiday by the sea great fun. Shells are not difficult to find and they are easy to keep once they have been cleaned. The study of seashells is called conchology. This is a world-wide activity but it can be started at your nearest beach.

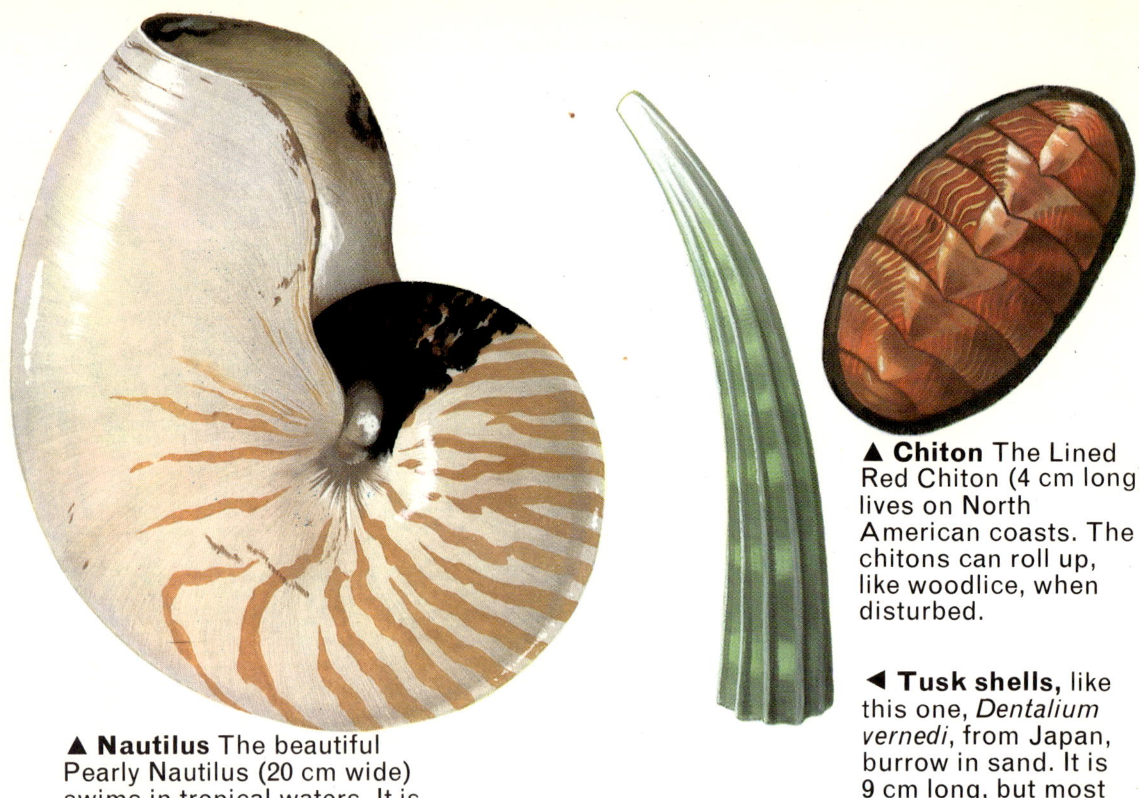

▲ **Nautilus** The beautiful Pearly Nautilus (20 cm wide) swims in tropical waters. It is related to octopuses, squids and cuttlefishes.

▲ **Chiton** The Lined Red Chiton (4 cm long), lives on North American coasts. The chitons can roll up, like woodlice, when disturbed.

◀ **Tusk shells,** like this one, *Dentalium vernedi*, from Japan, burrow in sand. It is 9 cm long, but most tusk shells are small and difficult to name.

What are Seashells?

Seashells are skeletons. Humans have skeletons inside their bodies, called internal skeletons, but many animals have skeletons outside their bodies. Shells are the hard outer coverings of animals which we call molluscs. Insects, crabs and sea urchins also have outer skeletons, and it is important not to mistake their skeletons for seashells.

The shells protect the molluscs' soft bodies from other animals and from the waves. Most molluscs live in the sea but some live on land and a few in fresh water.

The five major groups of molluscs are pictured on these two pages. There is also a sixth group which was only discovered in 1950. These rare cap-shaped shells are called *Neopilina*. It is unlikely that you will find any of these shells because they live in very deep waters.

The most common group of molluscs are the *gastropods*. Most gastropods have a single shell. This may be coiled, as in winkles and whelks, or dome-shaped as in limpets. The two-part shells, or *bivalves*, are the next largest group.

▶ **Scallop** The Noble Scallop (10 cm wide), from Japan, is one of the 20,000 species of bivalves in the world. Scallops usually live on the sea-bed. Many bivalves live in sand or mud.

▲ **Topshells**, like this *Calliostoma tigris* (5 cm high), from New Zealand, are gastropods. There are about 80,000 types of gastropods in the world. Many are found on rocks or stones.

The next three groups are not as common. Chitons, or coat-of-mail shells, are made up of eight separate plates. A few types of chitons have been found in deep water, but most are found on rocks close to the shore. Most tusk shells – shaped like the tusks of an elephant – also live in shallow waters. *Cephalopods* include the Nautilus, octopus, squid and cuttlefish. Of these, only the Nautilus has an outer shell. It lives in tropical waters and is quite rare. You are not likely to find it on your local beach. However, the 'bones' of its relative, the cuttlefish, can often be found on beaches all around the world.

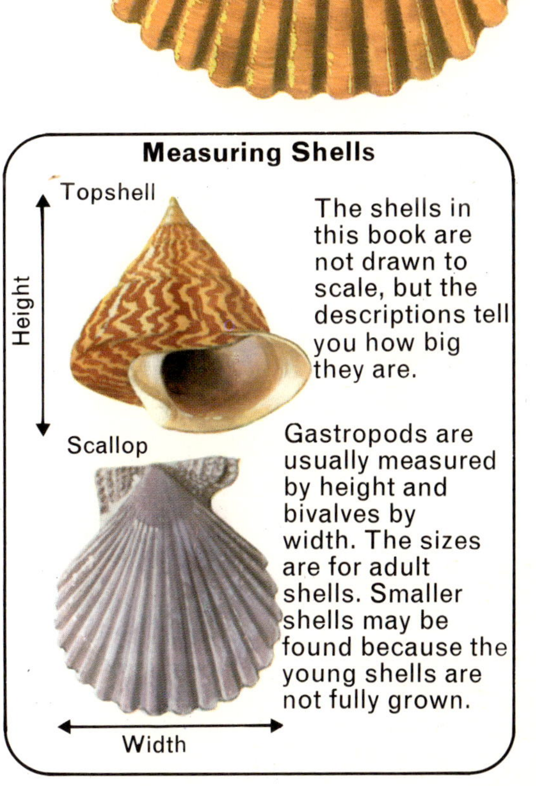

Measuring Shells

The shells in this book are not drawn to scale, but the descriptions tell you how big they are.

Gastropods are usually measured by height and bivalves by width. The sizes are for adult shells. Smaller shells may be found because the young shells are not fully grown.

How Shells are Made

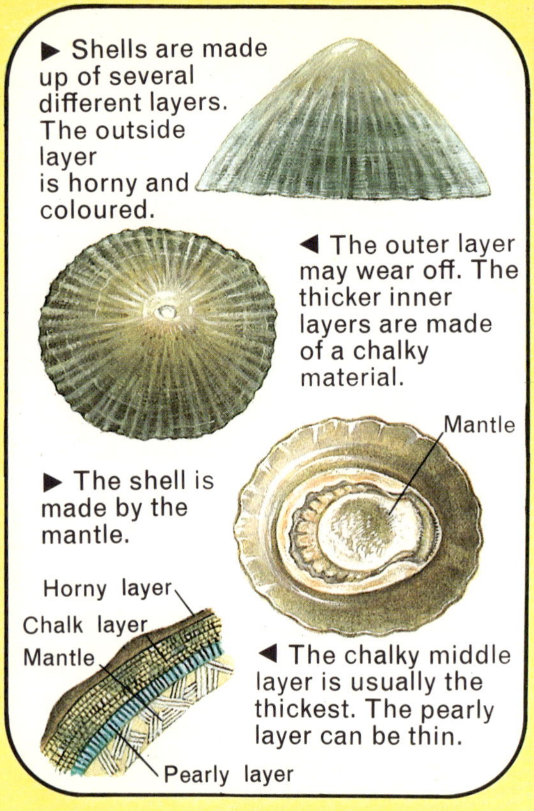

Molluscs grow shells rather as humans grow nails. The shell is produced by a fold of skin called the *mantle* and is built up in layers from it. The layers harden and are dead, just as the ends of nails are dead. Shell is made of a mixture of horn and chalky crystals which remains after the mollusc dies. The mollusc is attached to its shell by muscles.

The shell grows with the animal. The little whorls at the end of a Nautilus or winkle shell were made when the molluscs were tiny. Shells grow quickly when there is plenty of food and the water is warm. In cold water the shell grows slowly. The different growth rates cause ridges on the shell.

▼ **Bivalve shells**, like the Quahog, are usually joined at the hinge, or beak. There are teeth in the hinge. Sometimes it is possible to see the scars left by the muscles that held the shells shut. The Quahog has ridges across its shell. Some shells have ribs coming from the hinge.

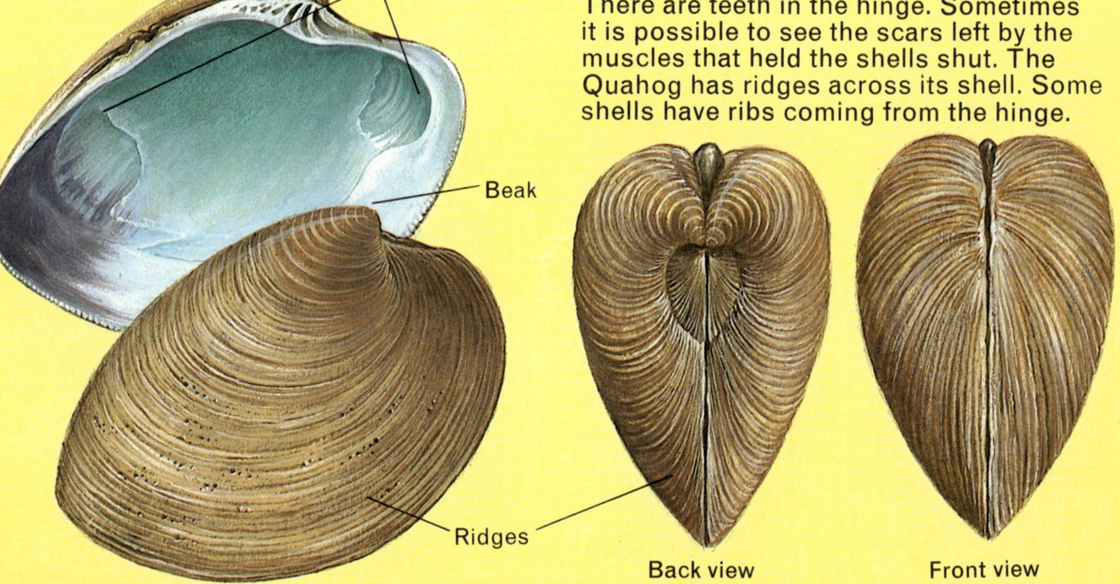

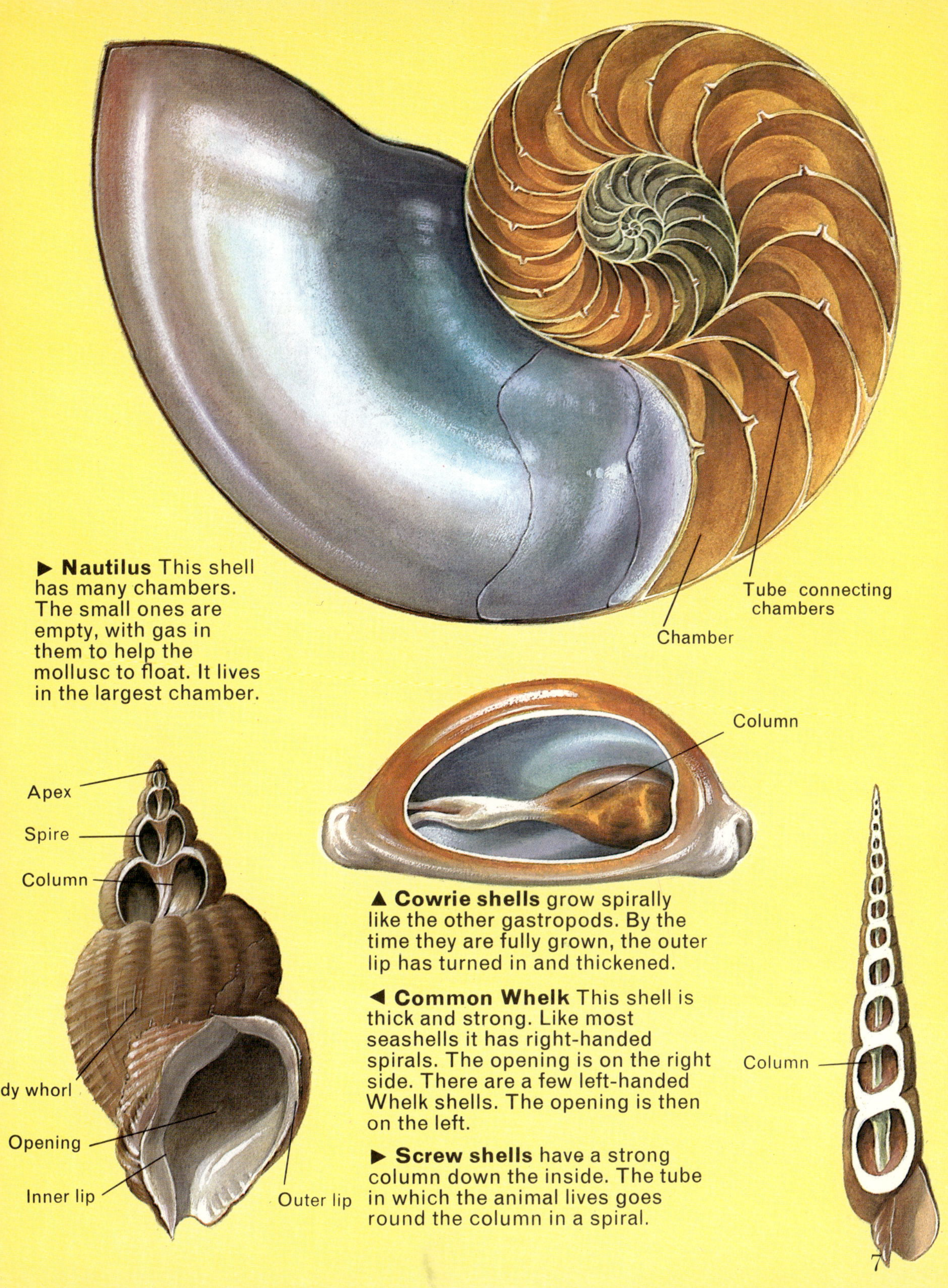

▶ **Nautilus** This shell has many chambers. The small ones are empty, with gas in them to help the mollusc to float. It lives in the largest chamber.

▲ **Cowrie shells** grow spirally like the other gastropods. By the time they are fully grown, the outer lip has turned in and thickened.

◀ **Common Whelk** This shell is thick and strong. Like most seashells it has right-handed spirals. The opening is on the right side. There are a few left-handed Whelk shells. The opening is then on the left.

▶ **Screw shells** have a strong column down the inside. The tube in which the animal lives goes round the column in a spiral.

What to Look For

Most of the shells you will find belong to the two main groups of shells – bivalves and gastropods. Some of the bivalves are shown below. Although these shells are in pairs when the mollusc is alive, the hinge usually breaks when it dies. So you will often only find one shell.

Some gastropod shells have a very simple form. Limpets are a flattened-cone shape. Slipper limpets are a little more complicated, with a small shelf on the inside. Some shells, like the ormers or abalones, have a line of holes along the top. The rest of the gastropods are much more complicated, with shells twisted into *whorls*. Some, like the winkles, have only a few whorls. Others, like the tower shells, have as many as 14.

Most gastropods have right-handed or *dextral* whorls, with the opening on the right. A few have openings on the left, with left-handed or *sinistral* whorls. These are much sought after by collectors.

Shells in Pairs

◀ **Venus shells** are oval, with hinges, curved sideways.

◀ **Cockles** are rounded, with a fan of ribs over them.

◀ **Razor shells** are long and thin and easy to recognize.

▲ **Carpet shells** have ridges and off-centre hinges.

▲ **Mussels** fasten themselves to rocks with fine threads.

◀ **Otter shells** are oval and ridged. There is a small pit inside the hinge of each shell.

▲ **Scallops** have broad ribs and 'wings' by the hinge.

Single Shells

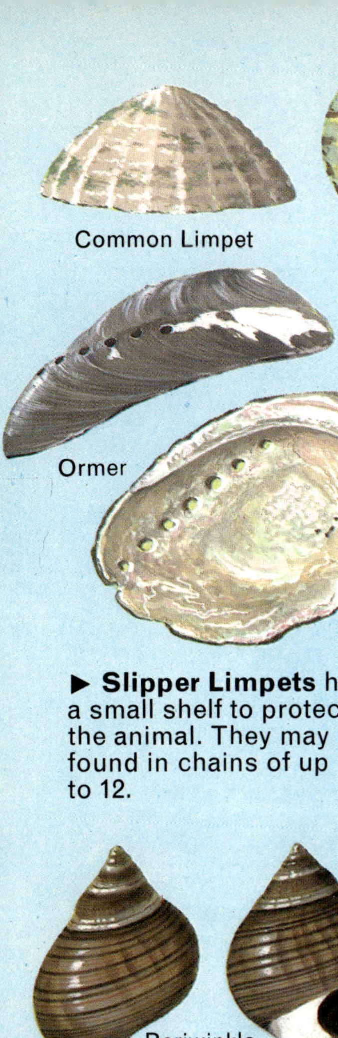

Common Limpet

White Tortoiseshell Limpet

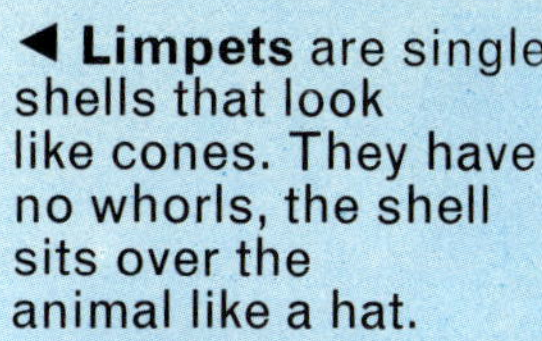

◀ **Limpets** are single shells that look like cones. They have no whorls, the shell sits over the animal like a hat.

Ormer

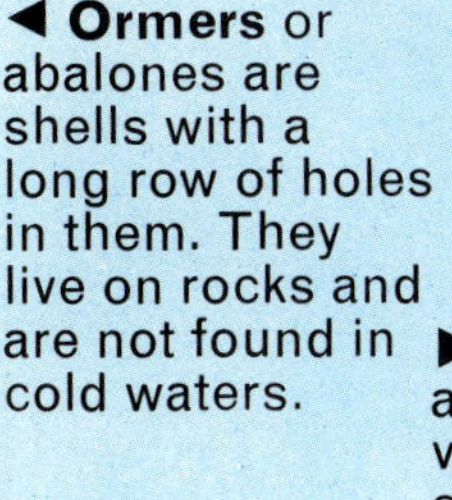

◀ **Ormers** or abalones are shells with a long row of holes in them. They live on rocks and are not found in cold waters.

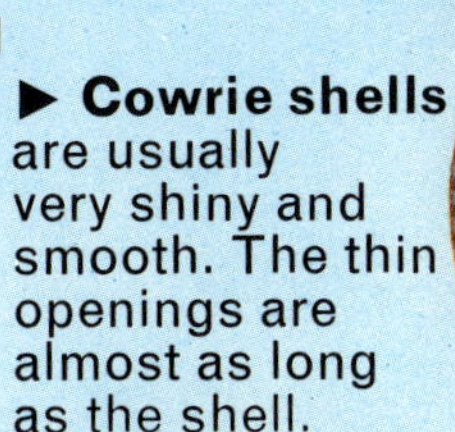

▶ **Cowrie shells** are usually very shiny and smooth. The thin openings are almost as long as the shell.

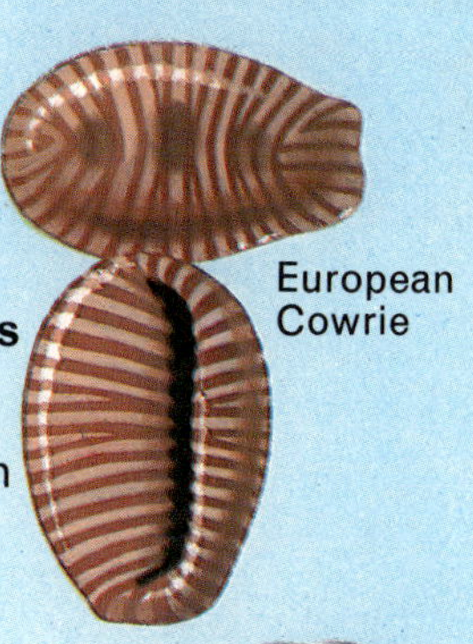

European Cowrie

Slipper Limpet

Chain living Slipper Limpets

▶ **Slipper Limpets** have a small shelf to protect the animal. They may be found in chains of up to 12.

◀ **Topshells and periwinkles** are cone-shaped, but with whorls. Periwinkles are more rounded than topshells and some are very small.

Periwinkle

Topshell

Needle Shell

Wentletrap

Tower Shell

Spire Shell

▲ **Tall, pointed shells** The number of whorls on these shells helps to tell which is which. Some have thicker ridges or ribs. Colours do not help as they vary from shell to shell.

Common Whelk

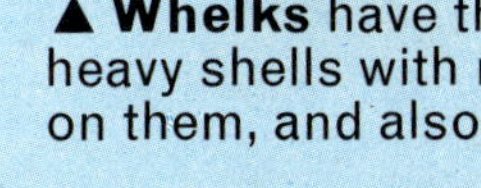

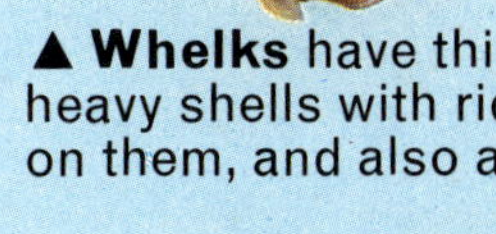

▲ **Whelks** have thick heavy shells with ridges on them, and also a lip.

Collecting Shells

Magnifying glass
Tape measure
Spade
Tablespoon
Shrimping net
Plastic boxes
Plastic bags
Bucket
Sieve

▲ Some of the things you will find useful for studying and collecting shells. It is sensible to wear old gym shoes, especially if you are looking on a rocky beach.

The best time for studying and collecting shells is at low tide, when the beaches are not covered by the sea. When you are exploring a beach, keep an eye on the time to make sure that you are not going to be cut off when the sea comes in. The equipment pictured left will be useful. But the most important thing to take with you is a notebook and pencil to record the type of shell you find.

On a sandy shore you can often find empty shells on the strand line – or high-tide mark. You will not find live molluscs here because it is too dry for them.

To study live molluscs on sandy or muddy shores, you will need to dig deeply with a spade at the low-tide mark. Fill a sieve with the sand

Keeping a Record

You should make full notes of all the shells you find. The notebook (left) shows you the sort of notes you should make. It is also useful to draw a picture of the shell. You can then put all your notes and drawings into a scrapbook (above) so that you have a record of all your findings.

or mud and wash it away. You may then find some bivalves left in the sieve. Take notes, and replace them. You can watch them digging back into the sand with their *foot*.

Studying molluscs is easier on a rocky shore because the animals cannot dig themselves in. Molluscs can be found sheltering under seaweed or in cracks and under rocks. A shrimping net is useful for exploring rock pools. Some molluscs live right at the top of a rocky beach in the upper shore. If you move rocks or stones to look under them, remember to replace them carefully. Be gentle too with the molluscs and put them back where you found them.

Empty shells can be washed in fresh water and brushed with a soft brush. They are then ready to be recorded and stored.

Where to Look

▲ **Sandy shores** are good places to look for shells, especially when the tide is out. You will find mostly bivalve shells.

▲ **Rocky shores** have many different kinds of shells clinging to the rocks. Look in crevices and cracks, and in pools.

▲ **Muddy shores** Low tide is the best time to search muddy shores and estuaries.

Storing Shells

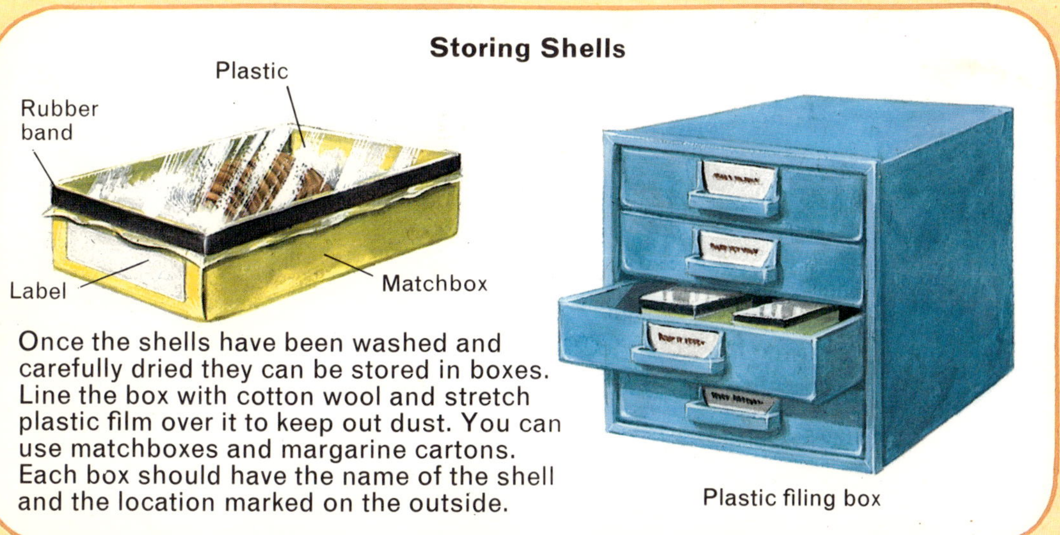

Once the shells have been washed and carefully dried they can be stored in boxes. Line the box with cotton wool and stretch plastic film over it to keep out dust. You can use matchboxes and margarine cartons. Each box should have the name of the shell and the location marked on the outside.

Shells on Sandy Beaches

Most of the shells found on sandy beaches are bivalves. The live molluscs are buried in the damp sand, away from the heat of the sun. They come up to the surface to feed when the tide comes in.

In deeper waters the molluscs do not have to burrow, because the tide does not uncover them. It is more difficult to collect shells from deeper waters. You will usually have to wait for the sea to wash them ashore. Some of the deeper water shells move about on the seabed quite quickly by shooting water from a tube called a *siphon*.

Some of the shells that can be found on sandy beaches are shown on these two pages. It is unlikely that all these shells will be found, and you may find some that are not illustrated here.

▼ **Tiger Scallop** (3 cm wide) It is not a beach shell but may be washed up.

▼ **Necklace Shell** (3 cm high) This shell may be washed up on the beach.

▼ **Common Whelk** (8 cm high) It is also found on rocky shores.

▲ **Common Cockle** (5·5 cm wide) Feeds at the surface and burrows in sand from the lower shore down.

▲ **Thin Tellin** feeding. Like cockles they burrow in the sand.

◀ **Prickly Cockle** (6 cm wide) Not common.

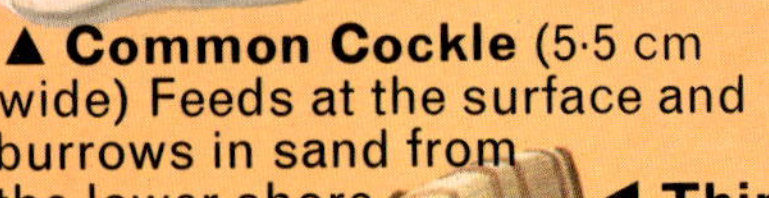

◀ **Thin Tellin** (2 cm long).

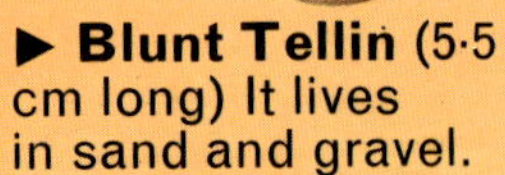

▶ **Blunt Tellin** (5·5 cm long) It lives in sand and gravel.

◀ **Common Otte Shell** (15 cm long Lives 30 cms or more below the surface.

Tides and Zones

Twice a day, the beaches are washed by the tides. Twice a month, when the moon is full or new, these tides rise very high and fall very low. These are the spring tides. Twice a month, when the moon is half full, the tides do not move up and down as far. These are the neap tides. The differences in the tides make zones on the beach.

The splash zone, at the top of the beach, is only covered by water at the highest spring tides. The upper-shore zone is the area between the high-water lines of the spring and neap tides. The lower shore is the area between the low-water lines of the spring and neap tides. The area in between is the middle shore.

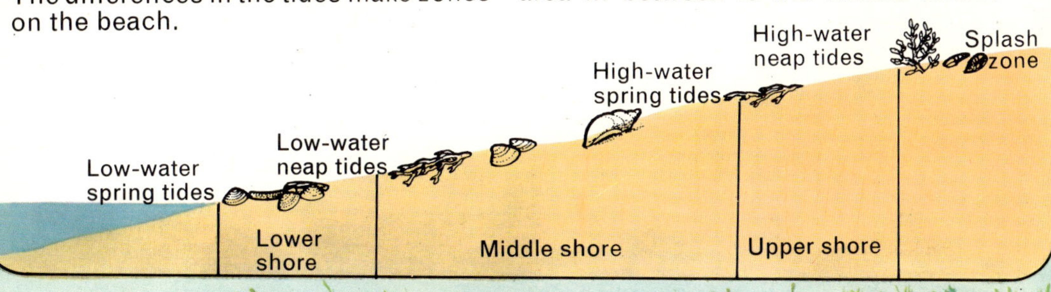

▶ **Dog Cockle** (6 cm wide) Burrows just below the surface and is often washed ashore.

▶ **Queen Scallop** (5-7·5 cm wide) It lives just below low tide mark.

◀ **Pelican's Foot** Shell (5 cm high) It is found on muddy gravel and on sand.

▼ **Rayed Artemis** (5 cm wide) Found in sandy bays on the lower shore and below.

▲ **Striped Venus** (3 cm wide) lives in the lower shore zone.

▲ **Banded Venus** (2·5 cm wide) It lives in the middle shore zone down to the sea.

▲ **Banded Wedge Shell** (3 cm long) It lives in the middle and lower zones of exposed shores.

▶ **Small Razor Shell** (10 cm long).

▲ **Rayed Trough** (5 cm wide) Usually lives just offshore.

◀ **Sand Gaper** (12 cm long) The two halves of the shell gape when closed.

◀ **Large Razor Shell** (15 cm long).

Rocky Shores

Most of the shells found on rocky shores are gastropods. The molluscs crawl over the surface of the rocks, scraping off the greenish film of algae or browsing on different kinds of seaweed. They scrape at food with their rough tongues. When the tide goes out, they clamp down onto the rock to keep in their body moisture.

Shells on rocky shores are exposed to the beating of the waves when the sea is rough, and they have to be able to stand up to the battering. Limpets can survive in very rough conditions, and they can be found everywhere. The molluscs which cannot grip the rock tightly will only be found in crevices on exposed shores.

Rock and Wood Borers

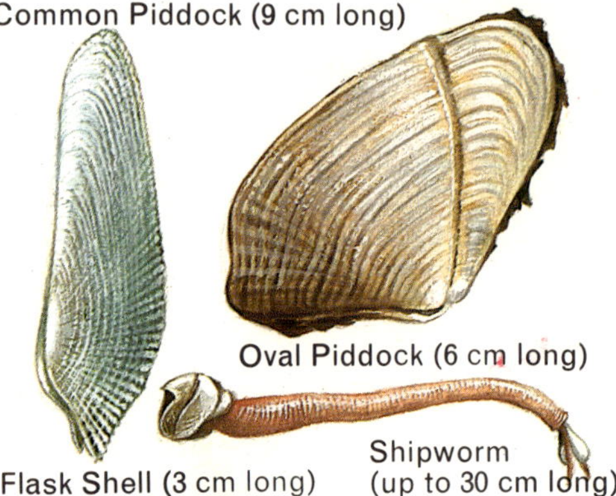

Common Piddock (9 cm long)

Oval Piddock (6 cm long)

Shipworm (up to 30 cm long)

Flask Shell (3 cm long)

Not all molluscs burrow into sand. A few bore into rocks and wood. The Shipworm bores into wood and causes a lot of damage to boats and piers. The Common Piddock is also found in wood, but it usually burrows in chalk or sandstone. The Oval Piddock is found in shale and clay. Flask Shells bore into sandstone or limestone.

▼ **Edible Periwinkles** (2·5 cm high) are a common species on the lower shore.

▼ **Painted Topshell** (2·5 cm high) It is pearly under the coloured horny layer.

▼ **Needle Shell** (1·2 cm high) It is found among stones and debris.

▶ **Keyhole Limpet** (1·5 cm high) It lives on lower shore rocks.

◀ **Chinaman's Hat** (2 cm high) It clamps on stones and other shells.

▶ **Common Wentletrap** (3·5 cm high) It has ribs that stand out and is found on the lower shore.

▶ **European Cowries** (4 cm long) are small and ribbed.

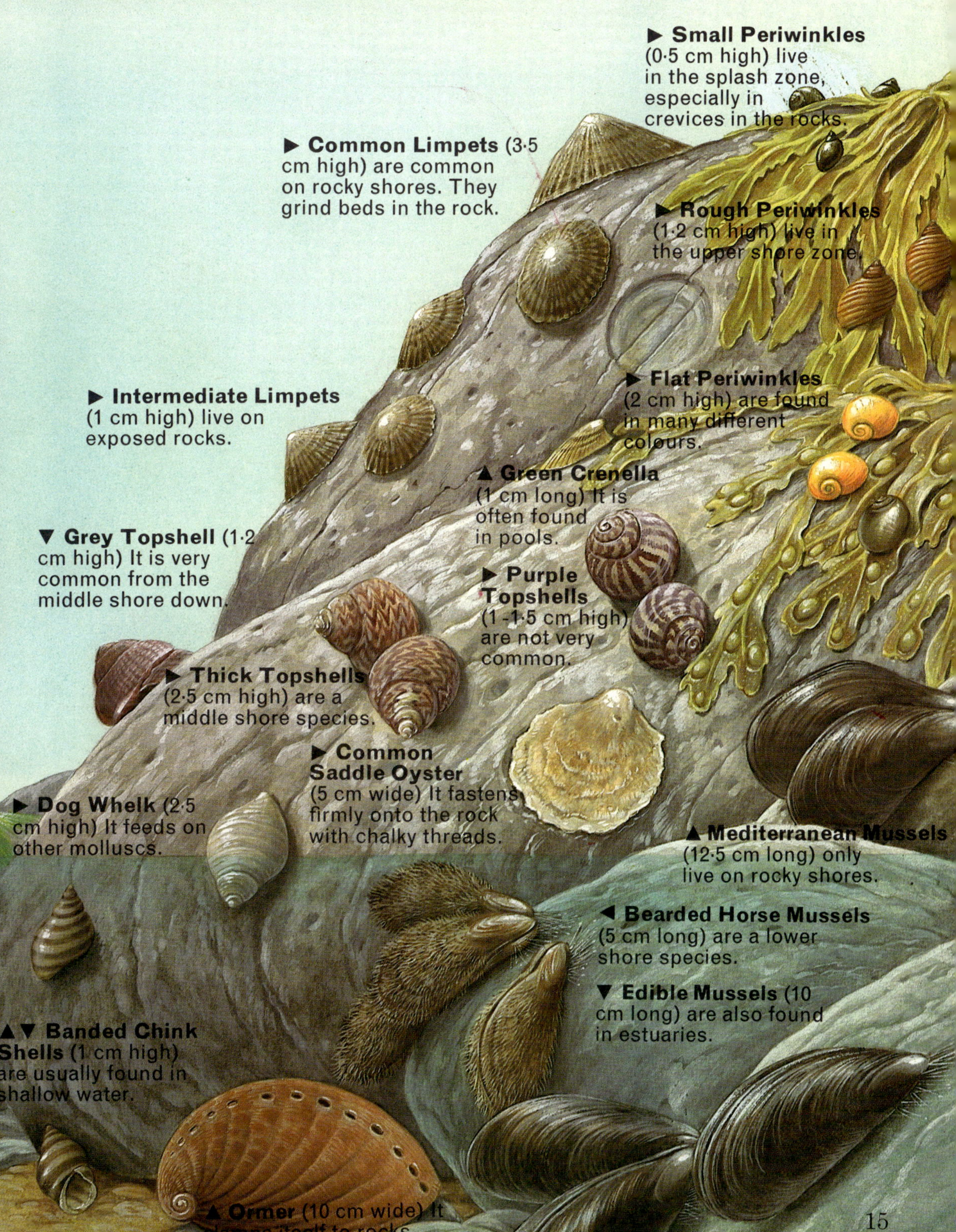
▶ Small Periwinkles (0·5 cm high) live in the splash zone, especially in crevices in the rocks.
▶ Common Limpets (3·5 cm high) are common on rocky shores. They grind beds in the rock.
▶ Rough Periwinkles (1·2 cm high) live in the upper shore zone.
▶ Flat Periwinkles (2 cm high) are found in many different colours.
▶ Intermediate Limpets (1 cm high) live on exposed rocks.
▲ Green Crenella (1 cm long) It is often found in pools.
▼ Grey Topshell (1·2 cm high) It is very common from the middle shore down.
▶ Purple Topshells (1-1·5 cm high) are not very common.
▶ Thick Topshells (2·5 cm high) are a middle shore species.
▶ Common Saddle Oyster (5 cm wide) It fastens firmly onto the rock with chalky threads.
▶ Dog Whelk (2·5 cm high) It feeds on other molluscs.
▲ Mediterranean Mussels (12·5 cm long) only live on rocky shores.
◀ Bearded Horse Mussels (5 cm long) are a lower shore species.
▼ Edible Mussels (10 cm long) are also found in estuaries.
▲▼ Banded Chink Shells (1 cm high) are usually found in shallow water.
▲ Ormer (10 cm wide) It clamps itself to rocks.

Estuaries and Muddy Shores

Estuaries are found where rivers run into the sea. Rivers carry soil which is deposited in the estuaries, making the shores muddy. These shores are washed by salt water when the tide is in, and by fresh water from the river when the tide is out. This makes an estuary a difficult place to live in.

There are, however, some advantages to life in an estuary. The river brings down plenty of food, so that these areas are quite well populated. As on a sandy shore, there are many bivalves. Some of them burrow in the mud. Others, such as mussels and oysters, grow on rocks or piers, fastened by short threads.

Apart from the seashells, there may be shells of freshwater molluscs which have been washed down stream. These freshwater shells are usually much thinner than seashells.

In the tropics, the estuaries often spread out into mangrove swamps. Many colourful molluscs are found there. Some are cemented to the roots of the mangrove trees and others crawl about on them, above the mud. The combination of warmth and plenty of food produces a large population of molluscs.

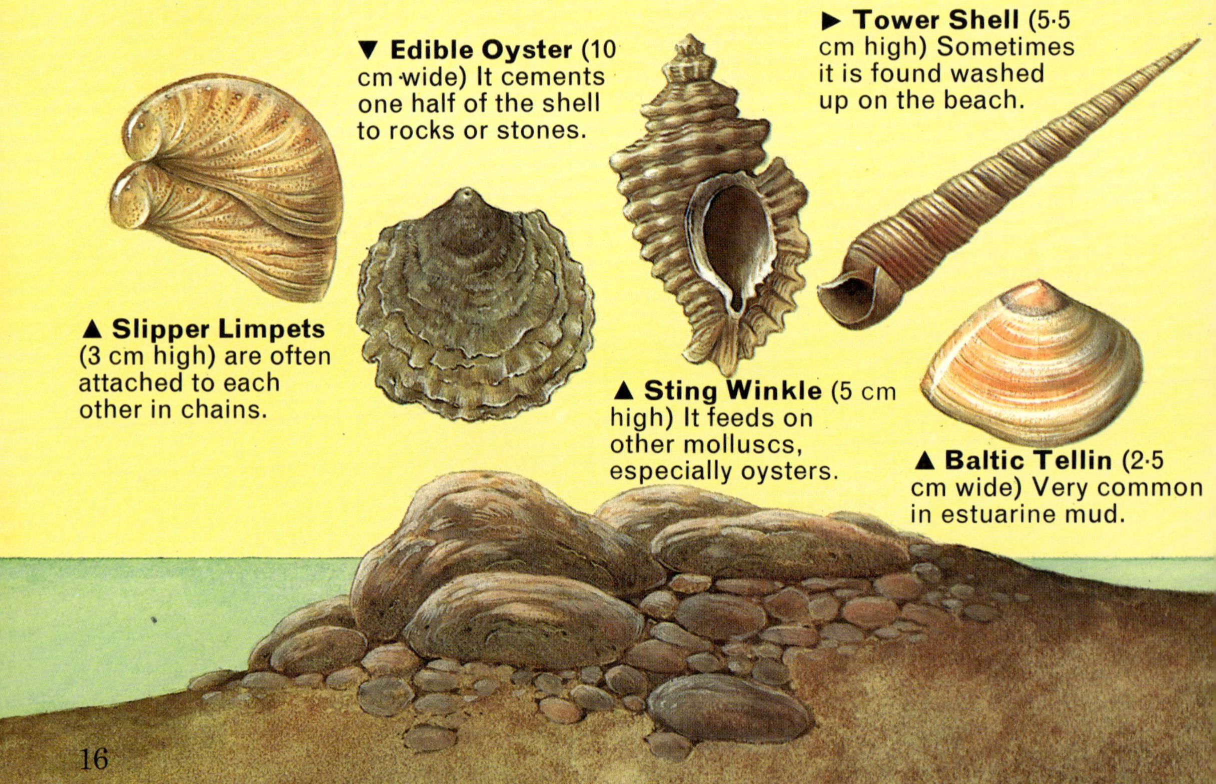

▼ **Edible Oyster** (10 cm wide) It cements one half of the shell to rocks or stones.

▶ **Tower Shell** (5·5 cm high) Sometimes it is found washed up on the beach.

▲ **Slipper Limpets** (3 cm high) are often attached to each other in chains.

▲ **Sting Winkle** (5 cm high) It feeds on other molluscs, especially oysters.

▲ **Baltic Tellin** (2·5 cm wide) Very common in estuarine mud.

Shells from Mangrove Swamps

Mangrove Cerith (4 cm high)

Telescope Shell (9 cm high)

Bleeding Tooth Nerite (2 cm high)

Mangrove Tellin (8 cm long)

Rough Winkle (2 cm high)

Mud Creeper (8–12 cm high)

American Crown Conch (10 cm high)

West Indian Crown Conch (10 cm high)

▼ **Spire Shell** (0·4 cm high) Smaller than the Laver Spire Shell, it has more whorls and a round opening. It is also numerous.

▲ **Laver Spire Shell** (0·5 cm high) It is very small and found in dense masses on mud-flats and salt marshes at low tide.

Freshwater Shells

Freshwater Winkle (3·5 cm high)

Freshwater Spire Shell (0·6 cm high)

Freshwater Nerite (0·6 cm high)

Freshwater Mussel (6–15 cm long)

Tropical Shells

The most beautiful shells are found in the warm waters of the Pacific and Indian Oceans. Shells grow faster in warm waters, so that the really large seashells are found in tropical coral reefs.

The largest seashell in the world is the Giant Clam, which lives in coral reefs around the Indian and Pacific Oceans. One of the rarest shells is the White-tooth Cowrie from deep waters near the Philippine Islands. The most expensive shell is also a tropical shell – the Bengal Cone – for which one shell collector paid £1350. It was trawled from the sea near Thailand.

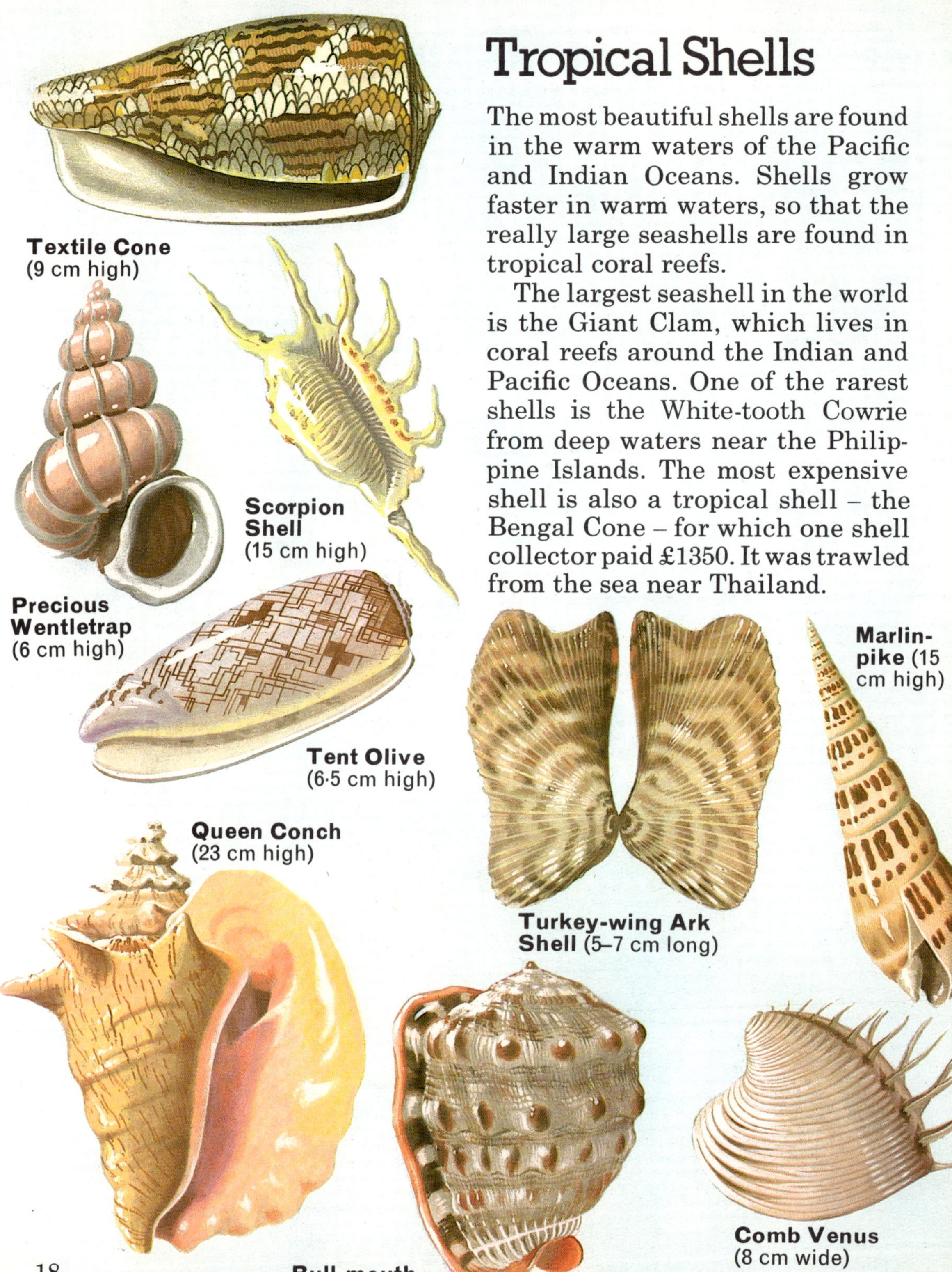

Textile Cone (9 cm high)

Scorpion Shell (15 cm high)

Precious Wentletrap (6 cm high)

Tent Olive (6·5 cm high)

Marlin-pike (15 cm high)

Turkey-wing Ark Shell (5–7 cm long)

Queen Conch (23 cm high)

Comb Venus (8 cm wide)

Bull-mouth Helmet (18 cm high)

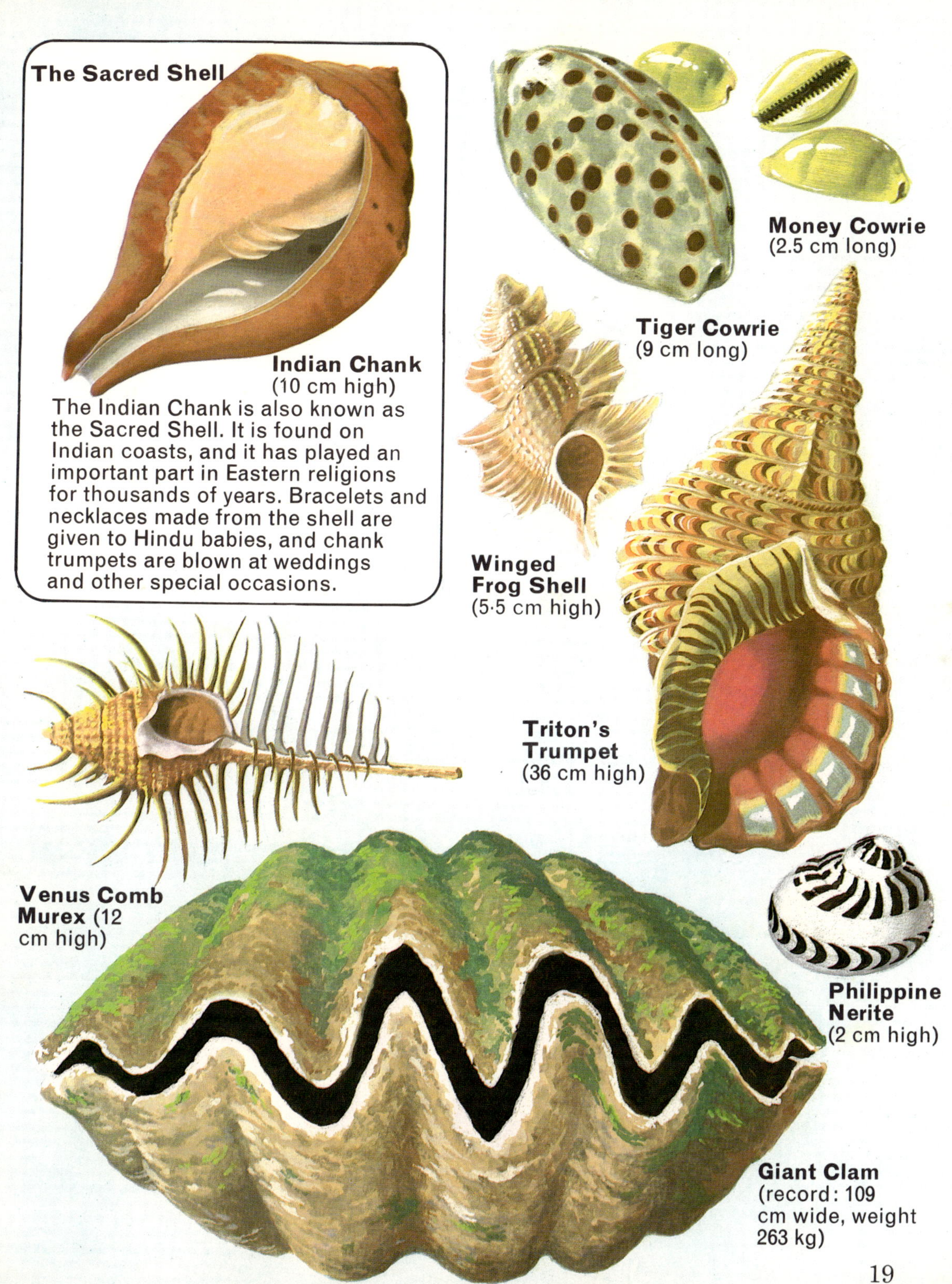
The Sacred Shell
Indian Chank
(10 cm high)
The Indian Chank is also known as the Sacred Shell. It is found on Indian coasts, and it has played an important part in Eastern religions for thousands of years. Bracelets and necklaces made from the shell are given to Hindu babies, and chank trumpets are blown at weddings and other special occasions.
Money Cowrie
(2.5 cm long)
Tiger Cowrie
(9 cm long)
Winged
Frog Shell
(5·5 cm high)
Triton's
Trumpet
(36 cm high)
Venus Comb
Murex (12
cm high)
Philippine
Nerite
(2 cm high)
Giant Clam
(record: 109
cm wide, weight
263 kg)

▼ **Cameos** are carved from shells, such as this Black Helmet Shell which lives in warm Mediterranean waters.

▲ **Byssus cloth** is made from the long silk-like threads of the Noble Pen Shell. The cloth was made into gloves and other garments.

▼ **Mother-of-pearl** is mac from the inside layer of many shells. These button were made from the Green Abalone.

Using Shells

Shells have many uses. Large tropical shells, like the False Trumpet, have been used for carrying water. Small Indian Chanks were used as babies' feeding bottles in India.

Some shells have been used as money. The Money Cowrie was so named because it was used as a coin in many parts of the world. The Quahog was cut into beads by the North American Indians. The beads, called wampum, were used like money.

A few bivalves fasten themselves to rocks with threads called byssus. Some of these threads are fine and silky and were used to weave fine cloth, rather like silk. The Noble Pen Shell, found in the Mediterranean Sea, was harvested in large numbers for its byssus.

Some molluscs have been valuable for the dye they produce. Two types of Mediterranean Murex produce a rich purple dye, called the Royal Purple. It was used to colour the borders on Roman senators' robes.

People have used shells as decoration and ornaments for thousands of years. Bracelets, necklaces and buttons have all been made from shells.

Shell money Money Cowrie shells (below), Wampum beads, made from the Quahog (above) and Tusk shells (left) were once used as money.

▲ **Sunset Tellin** In Victorian England, Sunset Tellins were popular for decoration.

▶ **Dye Murex** shells are attractive, but it is the mollusc inside that produces the valuable dye.

▲ **Windowpane Oysters** have thin clear shells, used to make lampshades.

Pearls, too, come from shells. The best pearls are produced by the Pearl Oyster, which lives in tropical waters. At one time Britain was famous for its freshwater pearls. The pearl is made when a tiny piece of grit irritates the soft tissue of the mollusc's mantle. The animal covers it with shell lining to protect itself, and this forms into a pearl.

Cameos are carved out of sea-shells. They are often made from helmet shells. The layers of these shells are different colours. The jeweller carves a design in the white layer and cuts around it down to the coloured layer.

Precious Pearls

In the past, the hundreds of Pearl Oysters, brought up from the sea-bed by Japanese divers gave just a few pearls. Today, there are Pearl Oyster farms in the warm waters around Japan. A bead is put into the oyster to start the pearl.

Things to Make

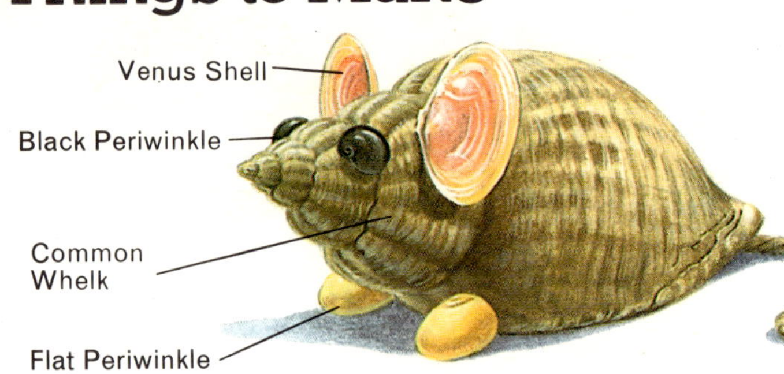

◀ **Shell animals** If you have a collection of different shells, you can use them to make shell animals. Whelks and limpets make a good start. See what you can invent. Stick the shells together with glue, allow the glue to dry and then cover the animal with a clear varnish.

You can use shells to make many different things. With a clear resin glue and bases that can be bought from handicraft shops, you can make very pretty brooches and earrings. Smaller shells can be strung into necklaces, using a needle and some fine nylon thread. Boxes can be decorated with shells, and different sized shells can be stuck together to make pictures or figures. Experiment with shells to make all sorts of patterns and shapes.

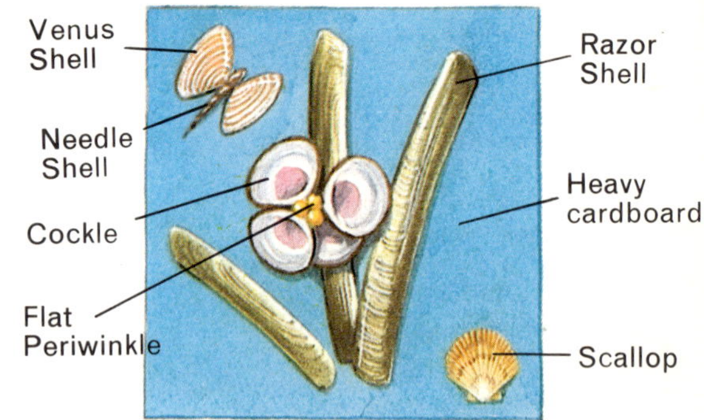

▲ **Shell pictures** You need a sheet of heavy card, some shells, clear glue and clear varnish. Arrange the shells on the card, then stick them down. You may want to paint the card first to show off the shells better. Varnish when the glue dries.

▶ **Shell brooch** Buy a brooch base, or make one by cutting a circle of card and sticking a safety pin to the back. Glue the first shell onto the middle and then arrange the other shells.

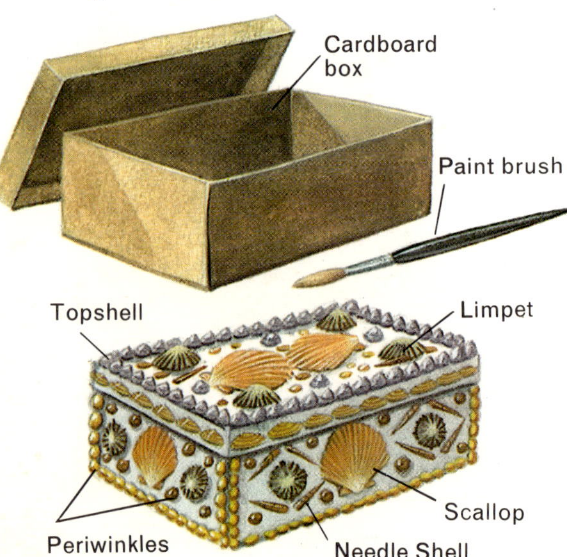

◀ **Shell boxes** Boxes decorated with shells make very good presents. They can be made as small as a matchbox or as big as a shoe box. Paint the box to cover any writing on it. Then carefully arrange the shells before you glue them onto the box. You could put a name on the lid in tiny shells. Leave enough space at the top of the box so that the lid will fit on. When the glue is dry, varnish the box and the shells.

Glossary

Aperture is the name given to the opening in a gastropod shell.

Apex The tip of the gastropod shell.

Base The broad end of a gastropod shell.

Bivalve or **Bivalvia** is the scientific name for molluscs with two shells, like clams.

Cephalopod or **Cephalopoda** is the scientific name for the Nautilus, the octopuses, squids and cuttlefishes.

Columella The central column in a gastropod shell.

Dextral shells are those with the aperture on the right. They are very common.

Foot describes the muscle with which a bivalve often digs and a gastropod moves.

Gastropod or **Gastropoda** is the scientific name for molluscs such as snails and limpets. These creatures have one shell or none.

Habitat describes the place in which a plant or animal lives. For example, a cockle's habitat is deep in the sand.

Lip The pearly edge of the aperture.

Mantle The fold of skin which covers the mollusc inside its shell, and from which the shell is made.

Radula The file-like tongue with which a gastropod scrapes at algae or drills into another mollusc's shell.

Sinistral shells are those with the aperture on the left. They are rare.

Siphons are the tubes with which molluscs breathe and feed. They draw in water through one siphon and squirt it out through another.

Spire The long, pointed part of a gastropod shell.

Valve is another name for a shell, in particular one half of a bivalve shell.

Whorl is the name of the twist in the tube of a gastropod. Different types of shells have different numbers of whorls.

Index

Books to Read

Shells of the World by A. P. H. Oliver (Hamlyn)
Seashells by S. Peter Dance (Hamlyn)
Seashells of the World by Gert Linder (Blandford Press)
The Life of Animals with Shells by Solene Whybrow (Macdonald Educational)
Seashells by R. Tucker Abbott (A Ridge Press Book, Bantam Books)
The Observer's Book of Sea and Seashore Edited by I. O. Evans (Warne)
Collins Pocket Guide to the Seashore by John Barrett and C. M. Yonge (Collins)